D0853668

Donated by:

REGIONS BANK

Summer Reading 2017

10 Things You Can Do To

Reduce, Reuse, and Recycle

by Elizabeth Weitzman

Content Consultant
Nanci R. Vargus, Ed.D.
Professor Emeritus, University of Indianapolis

Reading Consultant
Jeanne M. Clidas, Ph.D.
Reading Specialist

Children's Press®
An Imprint of Scholastic Inc.

Table of Contents

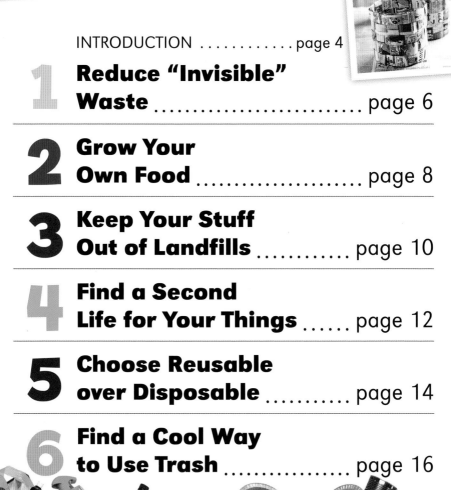

PLASTIC

METAL

2

GLASS

PAPER

Introduction

Clothes, toys, books, bags...we use so many different things every day! But what happens when we are done with them? If we throw them away, we **pollute** our Earth. And no one wants to live on a dirty planet. Do not worry. There are lots of things you can do to help.

Just remember the three Rs:

Reduce: Use only what you need.

Reuse: Use things more than once.

Recycle: Make old things new again.

1 Reduce "Invisible"

It is easy to see waste when you throw it in the trash. But there are some kinds of waste we cannot see. When we drive somewhere nearby, we waste gas. When we

Riding instead of driving doesn't just help the planet. It is good for you, too!

Waste

keep lights on in an empty room, we waste energy. You can reduce this waste! Walk or bike instead of riding in a car. Turn off the lights when you leave a room.

A shower is less wasteful than a bath. For one thing, you will use less water. For another, it will take less energy to heat the water. So...make your showers short!

Grow Your Own Food

Buying food from the grocery store creates waste. It takes a lot of energy to make food at a factory or farm. Plus, the trucks that bring the food to the store make the air dirtier. You can reduce a lot of that waste by growing your own fruits and vegetables.

Guess how far food travels from the farm to your plate. For some people it is an average of 1,500 miles (2,400 kilometers)! That is like driving from New York to Kansas just for dinner!

farmfoods
THE FROZEN FOOD SPECIALISTS

In a community garden, people plant their seeds together in a park. Maybe your town has one.

Keep Your Stuff

3

Did you know that the stuff you throw away winds up in a giant hole? It is called a **landfill**. Then the trash just sits there, making the Earth dirtier. The pile just gets bigger and bigger. Yuck! Our landfills are already overflowing. Think before you throw something away. Can you reuse it instead?

Out of Landfills

A bulldozer pushes trash around at an overflowing landfill.

Most people throw out more than 4 pounds (2 kilograms) of trash every day. By the end of a year, your trash could fill up your bedroom!

Find a Second Life

4

What do you do with clothes that no longer fit? Do you throw them away? Many people do. Four out

Do you have a lot of extra stuff you can donate?

for Your Things

of five pieces of clothing wind up in a landfill. There is a better way, though. Look for a charity that accepts used clothes. Or share your clothes with a friend! Do not throw away your clothes. There is always someone who can reuse them.

Most books are held together by glue. That is why they often cannot be recycled. Keep them out of landfills by setting up a book swap with a friend. When you finish your book, trade it for one your friend has finished.

5 Choose Reusable

Water bottles, juice boxes, plastic bags, and paper napkins. All of these are **disposable**. They create waste. Use cloth napkins

A reusable water bottle is an Earth-friendly choice!

over Disposable

that can be washed and reused. Use a reusable bottle or thermos for drinks. What other ideas can you think of?

If this sea turtle eats that plastic bag, it may choke.

People around the world use up to one _trillion_ plastic bags every year. And only one in 100 ever gets recycled. Unfortunately, a lot of them end up in the ocean. These bags hurt thousands of marine animals. Ask your parents to bring reusable bags to the store instead.

6 Find a Cool Way to

Many things that we throw away could be turned into something fun. This is called **upcycling**. Make origami art out

Origami is the Japanese art of folding paper into different shapes. You can use all sorts of paper to do it!

Use Trash

of paper that has already been used once. Turn a tin can into a pretty pencil cup—or even a bird feeder!

A few strips of felt turn an old can into a pretty pencil cup.

Dutch painter Enno de Kroon makes art, like these flowers, out of old egg cartons. He calls it eggcubism. His artworks have hung in museums. They have even sold for thousands of dollars!

7 Be Sure to Recycle

These backpacks are made from recycled plastic bottles.

Separate your paper, plastic, glass, and aluminum trash every day at home. Flatten boxes and wash out cans.

Plastic is not just recycled into new plastic bottles.
It can also be recycled into park benches, sleeping bags, backpacks, and... recycling bins!

Every Day

Your mom or dad can put all these items in bags. Then your town will collect it for recycling.

Some towns use special bags (above) for recyclables.

If Americans recycled every newspaper read, we would save about 250 million trees every year.

recycle

There are some things you cannot recycle at home. This includes computers, phones, and batteries. But don't throw them away! You can take them to a special recycling center. Ask your parents to find out when your town has an electronics recycling day.

In the United States, more than 100,000 cans are recycled every minute. Recycling one can can save enough energy to run a TV for two hours!

the Box

Yard waste can also be recycled. That includes leaves, branches, and grass clippings.

9 Compost Your

Compost is made from a mixture of decayed, or broken-down, natural materials, including food scraps. Yes, that sounds gross! But compost can be used to feed trees and plants. Ask your parents

Compost may not smell good. But it is great for the Earth!

Food Waste

if you can recycle your food by making a compost bin at home. Add your vegetable and fruit scraps to it after every meal. Then use the compost in your yard or at the park.

Every month, we each throw out about 20 pounds (9 kilograms) of waste that could have been composted. The plants in your garden would love that extra "food"!

Spread the Word

There are many ways you can teach people how to reduce, reuse, and recycle. Make sure your school has recycling bins like those below. Then explain to your friends why they should use the bins instead of a garbage can.

Your school should have bins for plastic, paper, metal, and glass.

PLASTIC

PAPER

METAL

GLASS

La Casa de Botellas means "the Bottle House" in Spanish. That is a good name for this house in Argentina. The walls are made of 1,200 plastic bottles. The doors and windows are made from 140 CD cases. And 320 bottles were used for the furniture. All of this is recycled! How long would it take you to save enough bottles to build a house like this?

Dress It Up: Project

Are you wondering if kids really can make a difference?

When Erek Hansen was 9 years old, he read about jeans that were recycled and used to help build homes after tornadoes and hurricanes. He asked around and found out that most people throw away their worn-out jeans and sneakers. So he started a yearly collection of denim and shoes. He calls his project Go Green Ohio. The denim from the jeans is used to rebuild homes that have been destroyed by storms.

Go Green

Some of the shoes go to people who need them. Others are recycled into sidewalks, carpets, and playgrounds. Erek has collected and recycled more than 35,000 items over the last five years! He helped set a Guinness World Record for "Largest Collection of Clothing to Recycle." And in 2015, he won the Presidential Environmental Youth Award (shown at left).

Pack an Earth-

Here are easy ways to reduce the amount of trash you generate every day.

Juice boxes will end up in the trash. Instead, pack a drink in a reusable bottle.

Rather than using plastic baggies for veggies and other snacks, ask your parents to buy reusable snack bags.

If you do have trash, make sure you recycle whatever you can. A paper lunch tray, a milk carton, and a plastic fork or spoon can all go in recycling bins.

Friendly Lunch!

If you bring your lunch to school in a paper bag, you will throw out as many as 20 bags a month! Bring a reusable lunch bag or a lunch box instead.

Don't wrap your sandwich in plastic or foil that will just be thrown away. Try a reusable sandwich wrap instead.

Glossary

- **disposable** (dih-SPOH-zuh-buhl): made to be thrown away after using

- **landfill** (LAND-fil): place where garbage is buried

- **pollute** (puh-LOOT): contaminate or make dirty

- **upcycling** (UP-sye-kling): turning something old into something new and better

Index

About the Author

Elizabeth Weitzman is a longtime journalist and the author of more than 25 nonfiction books for children. She and her family spend almost every weekend upcycling!

Facts for Now

Visit this Scholastic Web site for more information on how to reduce, reuse, and recycle:

www.factsfornow.scholastic.com

Enter the keywords Reduce, Reuse, and Recycle

Library of Congress Cataloging in Publication Data

Names: Weitzman, Elizabeth, author.
Title: 10 things you can do to reduce, reuse, and recycle / by Elizabeth Weitzman.
Other titles: Ten things you can do to reduce, reuse, and recycle
Description: New York, NY : Children's Press, an imprint of Scholastic, [2017] | Series: Rookie star. Make a difference | Includes index.
Identifiers: LCCN 2016003483 | ISBN 9780531226544 (library binding) | ISBN 9780531227602 (pbk.)
Subjects: LCSH: Recycling (Waste, etc.) —Juvenile literature. | Waste minimization—Juvenile literature. | Refuse and refuse disposal–Juvenile literature.
Classification: LCC TD792 .W394 2017 | DDC 363.72/82—dc23
LC record available at http://lccn.loc.gov/2016003483

Produced by Spooky Cheetah Press
Design by Judith Christ-Lafond

© 2017 by Scholastic Inc.

Photographs ©: cover grass: Anan Kaewkhammul/Shutterstock, Inc.; cover boy: IMAGEMORE Co, Ltd./Getty Images; cover yellow butterflies: kurga/Thinkstock; cover red butterflies: Cezar Serbanescu/Getty Images; cover newspapers: moodboard/Getty Images; cover sky: Elenamiv/Shutterstock, Inc.; 2 top: Alexandra Grablewski/MCT/Newscom; 2 recycling bins and throughout: Tomas Griger/Dreamstime; 2 bottom left plastic, 2 bottom right metal, 3 bottom left paper, 3 bottom right glass: RTimages/Fotolia; 4-5 background: patrick/Fotolia; 6-7 grass, 6-7 road: Iakov Kalinin/Shutterstock, Inc.; 6 bottom left: Christopher Futcher/iStockphoto; 6 bottom right: Ljupco Smokovski/Fotolia; 7 top right: Filipe B. Varela/Shutterstock, Inc.; 7 center right: Kuttelvaserova Stuchelova/Shutterstock, Inc.; 7 bottom left: greenland/Shutterstock, Inc.; 7 bottom center: MNStudio/Dreamstime; 7 bottom right: robert_s/Shutterstock, Inc.; 8: Justin Kase z12z/Alamy Images; 9: Susan Chiang/iStockphoto; 10-11 background: Sergey Zavalnyuk/Dreamstime; 11 bottom right: Deyan Georgiev/Shutterstock, Inc.; 12: Maxim Zarya/Thinkstock; 13: Wavebreakmedia Ltd/Dreamstime; 14: JAJIMO/Getty Images; 15 top: Stieber/Shutterstock, Inc.; 15 bottom: Norbert Wu/Superstock, Inc.; 16 bottom background: irynashumeika/Shutterstock, Inc.; 16 bottom: wckiw/Shutterstock, Inc.; 16 origami hat: aleksangel/Fotolia; 16 origami bird: NorGal/Shutterstock, Inc.; 17 top: Kelly Sillaste/Getty Images; 17 bottom: Enno de Kroon, Eggcubism; 18 yellow backpack: Courtesy of TerraCycle; 18 other backpacks: MCT/Newscom; 19 top: sebra/Shutterstock, Inc.; 19 bottom: Mike Watson/Thinkstock; 20: Mavor/Shutterstock, Inc.; 21: JupiterImages/Getty Images; 22 bottom left: 3445128471/Shutterstock, Inc.; 22-23 background: photka/Fotolia; 23 top: Christopher Hope-Fitch/Getty Images; 25: Alfredo Casa Ecologico; 26 inset, 26 background, 27: Amy Hansen; 28-29: Susan Swan/susanswan.com; 30 juice: mybaitshop/Fotolia; 30 lunch bag: Winai Tepsuttinun/Shutterstock, Inc.; 30 landfill: Sergey Zavalnyuk/Dreamstime; 30 plastic bags: Stieber/Shutterstock, Inc.; 30 pencil cup: Kelly Sillaste/Getty Images; 30 bottom left plastic, 30 bottom right metal, 31 bottom left paper, 31 bottom right glass, 32 left plastic, 32 right metal: RTimages/Fotolia.

32

PLASTIC

METAL